Table of Contents

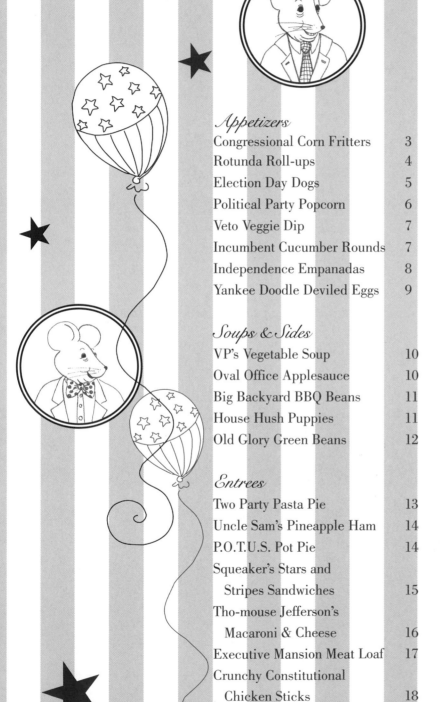

Welcome to Capital Cooking with Woodrow and Friends!

Woodrow G. Washingtail is President of the United Mice of America and the main character in our children's book, *Woodrow, the White House Mouse*, which teaches children about the presidency and America's most famous mansion. Woodrow's friends are other powerful members of the mouse government: Longworth McMouse, the "Squeaker of the House" (his human counterpart is the Speaker of the House), and Russell Mouse Bennett, the "Mouse-jority Leader" of the Senate (his human counterpart is the Majority Leader). They are both the main characters of *House Mouse, Senate Mouse*, which teaches young readers about Congress and the legislative process. And there is Marshall J. Mouse, the Chief Justice of the Supreme Court of the United Mice of America and the main character of *Marshall, the Courthouse Mouse*, which teaches kids about the judicial system, the Constitution and the Supreme Court. These books are available at your local bookstore (order by title), or you can order directly from us. Ordering information is on the copyright page.

Now join Woodrow, Longworth, Russell and Marshall in this cookbook for kids, as they whip up recipes for learning about our government and U.S. history, mixing fun facts with fun meals.

Peter & Cheryl

Peter and Cheryl Barnes

Appetizers

2 cups sweet corn

1/4 cup milk

1/3 cup flour

1 egg, beaten with fork

1/2 teaspoon salt

1/4 teaspoon pepper

2 tablespoons butter

2 tablespoons oil

Congressional Corn Fritters

You will need:

Skillet
Spatula
Spoon
Measuring cup and spoons
Paper towels

Combine the first six ingredients in a bowl. Stir to mix until blended. Melt butter and oil together in skillet over medium heat. Add corn mixture to skillet by rounded spoonfuls. Cook fritters for 3-4 minutes until golden brown on bottom. Gently flip with spatula and repeat until second side is golden brown, about 3-4 minutes. Remove fritters from skillet and drain on paper towels.

Makes 10-15 fritters, depending on size of spoonfuls.

Fun Facts

The Congress of the United States is made up of two elected bodies, the Senate and the House of Representatives. The Senate has 100 members; the House has 435. The most important job of Congress is to pass laws. A proposed law must be approved by both bodies.

Rotunda Roll-ups

You will need:

Knife
Bowl
Cutting board
Toothpicks
Plastic wrap
Platter

6 small flour tortillas

12 slices lunchmeat
   (ham, turkey, bologna,
   roast beef)

12 slices of your favorite
   kind of cheese

2 tablespoons mustard

2 tablespoons mayonnaise

Cut tortillas in half. In a small bowl, mix together mustard and mayonnaise. Spread a small amount of mustard mixture on each slice of lunchmeat. Set aside. Place a cheese slice on top of each tortilla half. Top with lunchmeat slice, mustard side up. Roll up from short end of tortilla and secure with a toothpick. Set on platter, cover with plastic wrap and refrigerate. Before serving, remove toothpicks.

Makes 12 roll-ups.

Fun Facts

The Rotunda is the great domed room in the center of the Capitol. The room is more than 96 feet in diameter and 183 feet high. Filled with many famous paintings and statues, it is used for ceremonial functions. Outside, on top of the dome, stands the 19 1/2 foot high Statue of Freedom.

4

Election Day Dogs

You will need:

Cutting board
Knife
Measuring spoons
Pastry brush
Cookie sheet

1 pkg. (8 rolls) refrigerated
   crescent style dinner rolls
4 hot dogs
4 slices American cheese
2 tablespoons milk
Sesame seeds

Unroll and separate rolls. Cut hot dogs in half to make eight small hot dogs. Slit hot dogs down middle. Cut cheese slices in half to make eight slices. Fold each cheese slice in half again and insert cheese into hot dog slit. Place each hot dog onto a crescent roll. Wrap roll around hot dog, rolling from large end of roll to small tip. Place cheese side up on ungreased cookie sheet. Brush with milk and sprinkle with sesame seeds. Bake at 375 degrees for 12-15 minutes until browned.

Makes 8 rolls.

Fun Facts

The President is elected every four years on the first Tuesday after the first Monday in November. There are elections every two years for all members of the House of Representatives. Senators are elected to six-year terms, with a third of the members elected every two years. On Election Day, voters go to "polling places" to cast their votes, or "ballots."

Political Party Popcorn

You will need:

13x9x2 baking dish
Saucepan
Measuring cup
Rubber spatula

Pour popped popcorn into 13x9x2 inch baking dish. Measure and add in peanuts but do not stir. Melt butter in saucepan over low heat. Remove butter from heat when melted and stir in honey with rubber spatula. Drizzle honey mixture over popcorn and peanuts. Stir gently until mixed using rubber spatula. Bake popcorn mix for 20 minutes in 300-degree oven, stirring gently twice. Remove from oven, loosen mixture and pour into bowl. Add raisins and pretzel sticks. Mix gently and serve.

Makes 6-7 cups.

Fun Facts

America is a democracy, and in democracies, people usually join political parties that represent their ideas and beliefs. The parties nominate candidates to compete against each other to continue or gain control of the government. In the United States, there are two major political parties, Democrat and Republican. But other independent parties are also growing.

6 cups popped popcorn

1 cup dry roasted peanuts

2 tablespoons butter

1/4 cup honey

3/4 cup raisins

1 cup pretzel sticks

6

Veto Veggie Dip

1 cup sour cream
1 cup mayonnaise
3/4 cup crumbled
   blue cheese
1 tablespoon apple
   cider vinegar
1 tablespoon lemon juice
1/2 tablespoon grated onion
1/2 teaspoon minced garlic
Black pepper to taste

You will need:

Spoon
Mixing bowl
Measuring cups and spoons
Grater for onion

Mix sour cream and mayonnaise in bowl. Add vinegar, lemon juice, onion and garlic. Mix. Gently fold in blue cheese. Add pepper if desired. You can dip your favorite veggies. Suggestions: carrot sticks, celery sticks, broccoli, cauliflower.

Fun Facts

When Congress proposes a law, the President must decide to approve or reject it. If he rejects it, that act is called a "veto."

When the 20th President, James A. Garfield, lived in the White House in 1880, he owned a dog named Veto.

Incumbent Cucumber Rounds

1 cucumber
1/2 cup white wine vinegar
1 cup water
8 oz. cream cheese, softened
1/4 cup mayonnaise
1/4 teaspoon garlic powder
1/4 teaspoon onion salt
Dash Worcestershire sauce
Sliced white bread

You will need:

Vegetable peeler
Knife
Round cookie cutter
Measuring cup
Measuring spoons
Bowl

Peel and slice cucumbers. Combine vinegar and water in a bowl. Add cucumbers to vinegar and water and let stand 2 hours. Drain cucumbers. Combine mayonnaise, garlic powder, onion salt, softened cream cheese and Worcestershire sauce. Mix well. Cut bread slices into rounds with cookie cutter. Spread cream cheese mixture onto one slice of bread. Top with a few cucumber slices. Top with another slice of bread.

Fun Facts

In an election, the incumbent is the politician who currently holds the office.

One president, Ulysses S. Grant, enjoyed eating cucumbers soaked in vinegar for breakfast when he was a general during the Civil War.

Independence Empanadas

You will need:

Cookie sheet
Fork
Large round cookie cutter
(approx. 3-4 inches in diameter)

1 lb. ground beef
1 package taco seasoning mix
1 cup shredded cheddar or
Mexican flavored cheese
2 boxes (2 sheets each box)
prepared pie crust sheets
Salsa for dipping

Brown ground beef and drain. Add taco mix and prepare as directed on package. Unfold piecrusts and cut out large circles (about 4 per sheet). Place a spoonful of beef mixture on one half of the piecrust circle. Sprinkle with cheddar or Mexican cheese. Fold piecrust over to cover ground beef and cheese. Press edges with fork to seal. Place on cookie sheet. Use piecrust directions to determine oven temperature. Bake for 10 minutes until browned. Serve with salsa for dipping.

Makes 16 empanadas.

Fun Facts

The Declaration of Independence was approved on July 4, 1776, by the Founding Fathers in the Continental Congress. Independence Day is our nation's birthday. It is celebrated with parades, picnics and fireworks. But it was not declared a national holiday until 1941. Only two Founding Fathers who signed the Declaration of Independence later became presidents: John Adams and Thomas Jefferson.

Yankee Doodle Deviled Eggs

6 eggs

1 teaspoon yellow mustard

2 1/2 tablespoons mayonnaise

1/4 teaspoon salt

1/4 teaspoon pepper

1/2 tablespoon pickle relish

Paprika

You will need:

Saucepan
Bowl
Fork
Measuring spoons
Spoon

Place eggs in saucepan and cover with cold water. Bring eggs to a boil over medium heat. Reduce heat and simmer for 15 minutes. Remove from heat and place saucepan in sink under cold water. Run water over eggs until cool to the touch. Remove eggs and dry. Remove shells from eggs. Slice eggs in half lengthwise. Put yolks in bowl. Mash yolks with fork. Stir in mayonnaise, mustard, salt, pepper and pickle relish. Mix until smooth. Spoon yolk mixture into egg white halves. Sprinkle with paprika.

Makes 12 deviled eggs.

Fun Facts

"Yankee Doodle" is a song popular in the U.S. since colonial times. "Yankee Doodle Dandy" and other words in the song were written by an English doctor to make fun of untrained American soldiers. But the soldiers liked the song and eventually adopted it as their anthem.

Soups & Sides

1 medium onion, sliced

2 celery stalks, sliced

1 can potato chunks, drained

1 can corn, drained

1 can peas and carrots, drained

2 tomatoes cut into chunks

3 tablespoons butter

3 tablespoons flour

4 cups tomato juice

2 cups water

1 tablespoon salt

1/2 teaspoon pepper

1/2 cup alphabet macaroni

VP's Vegetable Soup

You will need:

Measuring cup and spoons
Soup pot
Knife
Cutting board

Slice onion and celery. In soup pot, melt butter over medium heat. Add onion and celery and cook for 10 minutes, stirring until soft. Add flour and stir for one minute. Add tomato juice, water, salt, pepper and macaroni. Stir well. Add potatoes, corn, peas, carrot and tomatoes. Cook soup over medium heat, until just boiling. Reduce heat and simmer about 20 minutes until hot.

Fun Facts

"VP" stands for vice president, the number two position in the U.S. government behind the president. Of the 45 vice presidents who have served in office, only 12 have gone on to become president.

4 red apples, your favorite
    variety

1/4 cup apple juice

2 teaspoons lemon juice

1/4 cup honey

Pinch of ground cinnamon

Pinch of nutmeg (optional)

Oval Office Applesauce

You will need:

Blender or food processor
Vegetable peeler
Apple corer
Knife
Measuring cup and spoons

Peel, core, and cut apples into small chunks. Place chunks in blender or food processor, with apple juice, lemon juice and honey. Blend until smooth. Chill or serve at room temperature sprinkled with cinnamon and nutmeg.

Makes approximately 5 servings.

Fun Facts

The Oval Office is the president's main, formal office in the White House (he also works in a private study just off the Oval Office). The Oval Office was originally built in the center of the West Wing of the White House in 1909. In 1934, it was moved to the southeast corner of the West Wing. Each president decorates the office in his own style.

Big Backyard BBQ Beans

16 oz. can brick
    oven-baked beans
1 small onion sliced into rings
1/2 teaspoon dry mustard
1/4 cup packed brown sugar
1/4 cup ketchup
1/4 cup BBQ sauce
    (Marshall likes to use "U.B.
    the Judge"® BBQ Sauce)

You will need:

Spoon
Measuring cup and spoons
Baking dish
Knife

Preheat oven to 325 degrees. Arrange onion slices on bottom of baking dish. Add beans and remaining ingredients. Stir until mixed. Bake uncovered until bubbly about 30-35 minutes.

Makes 4-6 servings.

Fun Facts

The Big Backyard is the name some people give for the large South Lawn of the White House. On the grounds of the lawn are a tennis court, swimming pool and many gardens, including the famous Rose Garden, where presidents often make important announcements or greet famous visitors. And it is the site of the annual Easter Egg Roll, a treat for thousands of children.

House Hush Puppies

(Vegetable oil for frying)
2 cups white cornmeal
1 tablespoon all-purpose flour
3/4 teaspoon baking soda
1 teaspoon salt
1 teaspoon baking powder
1 cup buttermilk
1 small onion finely chopped
1 large egg, beaten

You will need:

Heavy skillet or deep fryer
Measuring cup and spoons
Tablespoon
Paper towels
Spatula

Heat oil over medium-high heat or until fryer registers about 375 degrees. Combine first five ingredients in a large bowl. Stir in buttermilk and onion, then add egg. Mix well. Drop batter by tablespoon into oil. Do not overcrowd. Cook until golden brown about 3-4 minutes, turning if needed. Remove from oil and drain on paper towels. Serve warm.

Fun Facts

The House of Representatives is made up of 435 members, with representation based on population of the various states. A few states with small populations, such as Wyoming, have only one representative. California, the most populous state, has the most representatives, 52.

Old Glory Green Beans

You will need:

Saucepan
Water
Measuring spoons
Spoon

1 lb. green beans
2 tablespoons butter
1 tablespoon balsamic vinegar
Salt to taste
Parmesan cheese, grated

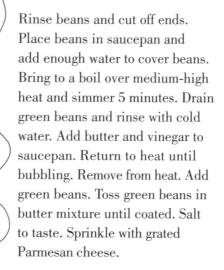

Rinse beans and cut off ends. Place beans in saucepan and add enough water to cover beans. Bring to a boil over medium-high heat and simmer 5 minutes. Drain green beans and rinse with cold water. Add butter and vinegar to saucepan. Return to heat until bubbling. Remove from heat. Add green beans. Toss green beans in butter mixture until coated. Salt to taste. Sprinkle with grated Parmesan cheese.

Makes about 4 servings.

Fun Facts

"Old Glory" is another name for the U.S. flag. A sea captain, William Driver, gave the flag that name. When Driver received command of his first ship, his family gave him a flag as a gift. He flew it on his ship on his trips around the world.

Entrees

6 cups water

6 oz. spaghetti

2 tablespoons butter

2 eggs, beaten with fork

1/3 cup grated
Parmesan cheese

1/2 pound ground
beef or turkey

1 small onion, chopped

1 8 oz. jar pizza sauce

1 cup mozzarella cheese,
shredded

Two Party Pasta Pie

You will need:

Measuring cup   Spatula
Saucepan   9-inch pie plate,
Colander   greased
Mixing bowl   Knife
Measuring spoons

Bring water to a boil. Add spaghetti. Cook for 10-12 minutes, or until just tender. Drain spaghetti. Put spaghetti into a large mixing bowl. Add butter and mix until melted. Stir Parmesan cheese into the beaten egg. Pour egg and cheese mixture over spaghetti and mix well. Grease pie plate on sides and bottom. Pour spaghetti mixture into pie plate and press up the sides with the back of a spoon to form a "crust." Brown ground meat and chopped onion until no longer pink and onion is soft. Drain grease from pan. Add pizza sauce and mix well. Spoon meat mixture onto the spaghetti crust. Spread evenly over the center of the crust. Bake pie at 350 degrees for 20 minutes. Remove from oven and sprinkle with mozzarella cheese (over meat mixture). Bake until cheese is melted, about 5 more minutes. Let pie stand 5 minutes then cut into pie slices.

Makes 6-8 servings.

Fun Facts

The United States has two major political parties, Democrat and Republican. But there have been plenty of other parties, large and small. Teddy Roosevelt sought re-election to the presidency in 1912 through the Progressive (or "Bull Moose") Party. Other third parties in American history include the Free Soil Party, the Greenback Party and the Farmer-Labor Party.

Uncle Sam's Pineapple Ham

6 slices canned ham
   (each about 1/2 inch thick)
1 can crushed pineapple
   with syrup
1/3 cup brown sugar
1 tablespoon vinegar
3 tablespoons mustard

You will need:

Glass baking dish
Can opener
Measuring cup and spoons

Place ham slices in baking dish.
Mix pineapple, brown sugar,
vinegar and mustard. Spoon over
ham slices. Bake at 350 degrees
for 45 minutes, basting occasionally
with glaze from dish.

Makes 6 servings.

Fun Facts

"Uncle Sam" is a fictional
character that symbolizes
the United States. The
name came from the War
of 1812, when it arose
as an unfriendly nickname
for the U.S. government.
"Uncle Sam" may have
come from the letters "U.S."
that were imprinted on
government property and
uniforms.

P.O.T.U.S. Pot Pie

3 cups cooked turkey, diced
3/4 cup milk
1 cup chicken broth
1 can mixed vegetables,
   drained
1 can cream of chicken soup
1 egg, beaten
1/4 cup cornmeal
3/4 cup biscuit mix

You will need:

Saucepan
9x13 baking dish
Fork
Large bowl
Measuring cup

Combine turkey, chicken broth and
soup in a saucepan. Bring to a boil.
Remove from heat and stir in vegetables. Pour mixture into baking dish.
In a large bowl, mix biscuit mix,
cornmeal, egg and 3/4 cup milk. Mix
with fork until smooth. Pour biscuit
mix over turkey mixture. Bake at
350 degrees for 25 minutes until
browned and bubbly.
Makes 4-6 servings.

Fun Facts

P.O.T.U.S. are the initials
for the most powerful posi-
tion in the world, "President
Of The United States."
The phrase is pronounced
"PO-tus." Within the White
House, it is a nickname for
the president used by the
Secret Service, news media
and White House staff.

The Squeaker's Stars and Stripes Sandwiches

For the stars:

White sandwich bread
   (2 slices per star)
Bananas (1/2 per sandwich)
Peanut butter

For the stripes:

White sandwich bread
   (4 slices per flag)
Peanut butter
Jelly, strawberry or grape

You will need:

Star-shaped cookie cutter
Knife
Wax paper or plastic wrap
Cutting board

For the stars: Spread peanut butter on one slice of bread. Slice the banana and arrange slices on top of peanut butter. Spread second piece of bread with peanut butter and place on top of bananas. Use star-shaped cookie cutter to shape.

For the stripes: Spread peanut butter on one piece of bread. Top with another plain piece of bread. Spread top of plain piece with jelly. Top with another plain piece of bread. Spread top of plain piece with peanut butter. Top with the final piece of bread. Trim off all crusts. Wrap sandwich in wax paper or plastic wrap. Chill for 2 hours. Unwrap the stack and slice vertically into four strips. Lay strips on their sides to make flags.

Serve with stars.

Fun Facts

"Squeaker" is a play-on-words of the term "Speaker of the House." The Speaker presides over the House of Representatives. He is usually the leader of the party in control of the House. His major powers are assigning bills to committees for review and controlling debate on the floor by granting the right of a member to speak.

The "Stars and Stripes" is the most popular name for the nation's red, white and blue flag.

15

Tho-mouse Jefferson's Macaroni & Cheese

You will need:

Measuring cups and spoons
Saucepan
2 quart casserole, greased

2 cups elbow macaroni

1/4 cup butter

1/4 cup all-purpose flour

2 1/2 cups milk

1 teaspoon salt

1/2 teaspoon pepper

2 cups shredded cheese,
    divided (your favorite kind)

3 slices bread

Cook pasta about 5 minutes, drain. In saucepan, melt butter over medium heat. Blend in flour, salt and pepper. Add milk gradually while stirring. Bring to a boil, stirring constantly, until sauce thickens. Remove from heat. Stir in 1 3/4 cups shredded cheese until melted. Add macaroni. Pour macaroni mixture into 2 quart greased casserole dish. Crumble bread slices on top of macaroni. Sprinkle with remaining 1/4 cup shredded cheese. Bake uncovered in 375-degree oven for 25-30 minutes until browned and bubbly.

Makes 4-6 servings.

Fun Facts

Thomas Jefferson, the third president, is credited with introducing macaroni to the United States. He brought the first macaroni machine home with him from France, where he served as U.S. Ambassador after the American Revolution.

"Macaroni" was the name of the pony owned by President Kennedy's daughter, Caroline. The pony received thousands of fan letters from children across the nation.

Executive Mansion Meat Loaf

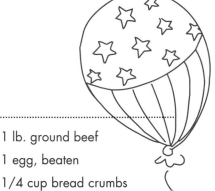

You will need:

Baking dish
Measuring cup
Measuring spoons
Knife

1 lb. ground beef

1 egg, beaten

1/4 cup bread crumbs

1/2 tablespoon mustard

1 tablespoon minced onion

1/2 cup ketchup

1/2 tablespoon
    Worcestershire sauce

1/4 cup mozzarella
    cheese, shredded

1/2 teaspoon salt

1/2 teaspoon pepper

Glaze:

1/4 cup ketchup

1 tablespoon oil

1 tablespoon brown sugar

1 teaspoon Worcestershire sauce

Mix all ingredients for meatloaf together in a large bowl until blended – your hands will work best! Form meat mixture into a loaf shape and place in baking dish. Mix together ingredients for the glaze. Spread with knife on top of meatloaf, like frosting a cake. Bake in 350-degree oven for 50 minutes or until no longer pink.

Makes 4-6 servings.

Fun Facts

The White House wasn't always called "The White House." In the 1800's, it was called "The Executive Mansion" or "The President's House." Teddy Roosevelt officially named it "The White House" when he became president in 1901. The only president who did not live in the mansion was George Washington, because it was not finished until after he left office.

2/3 cup bread crumbs

2/3 cup grated
   Parmesan cheese

1/4 teaspoon salt

1/8 teaspoon pepper

2 eggs, beaten

2-3 pounds chicken
   drumsticks

Crunchy Constitutional Chicken Sticks

You will need:

Shallow bowls (2)
Baking sheet
Aluminum foil
Fork
Measuring cup
Measuring spoons

In shallow bowl, mix together first four ingredients. Set aside. Beat eggs with fork in separate dish. Dip chicken in egg, one piece at a time, then roll in breadcrumb mixture. Place chicken legs skin side up on foil-lined baking sheet. Bake in 350-degree oven for one hour.

Fun Facts

The Constitution, adopted in 1787, created the American form of government, with three separate but equal branches (executive, legislative, and judicial) and a balance between state and federal powers. Only two men who became president signed the Constitution: George Washington and James Madison. Madison is considered the "Father of the Constitution." He led the Founding Fathers in forming the major provisions of the document, as well as the Bill of Rights.

Presidential Pork Chops

You will need:

Large bowl
Measuring cup and spoons
Skillet

1/3 cup Italian salad dressing

2 tablespoons brown sugar

2 teaspoons yellow mustard

4-6 pork chops, boneless, any
   thickness you want.

Mix together in large bowl salad dressing, brown sugar and mustard. Add pork chops and marinate for 1-2 hours. Heat skillet over medium high heat. Add pork chops. Discard left-over marinade. Pan fry pork chops, turning until browned and no longer pink inside.

Cooking time will depend on thickness of pork chops. For thin-sliced, approximately 4-5 minutes per side. For thicker cuts, slice chops in middle to create "butterfly" chops. Brown center for 3 minutes and turn over. Cook 7-8 minutes per side.

Makes 4-6 servings.

Fun Facts

The word "president" comes from the Latin word "praesidens," meaning "to preside."

Abraham Lincoln had a pet pig as a child. Theodore Roosevelt owned a pet pig for his children while the Roosevelts lived at the White House.

Salads

Woodrow's "Eggs"ecutive White House Salad
With Red, White & Blue Cheese Dressing

You will need:

1 lb. fresh baby spinach
   (comes washed and bagged
   at your supermarket)
1/4 cup sliced red onion
1/2 cup chopped
   hard-boiled egg
1/2 cup prepared bacon pieces
3 oz. crumbled bleu cheese
2 1/2 tablespoons red
   wine vinegar
1/2 cup olive oil
1/2 teaspoon Dijon mustard
Salt and pepper to taste

Small saucepan and water
Knife
Measuring cup
Large salad bowl
Measuring spoons
Bowl

To hardboil eggs: Place eggs (in shell) in saucepan and cover them with cold water. Bring water and eggs to a boil over medium heat. Reduce heat and simmer for 15 minutes. Rinse eggs with cold water and cool completely. Remove from shell and chop. Arrange spinach in salad bowl or on large platter. Add red onion and toss. Sprinkle bacon pieces, chopped egg and 2-oz. bleu cheese over spinach and onion. Mix oil, vinegar and mustard in bowl until blended. Add remaining bleu cheese and salt and pepper to taste. Pour dressing lightly over salad. Serve immediately and pass remaining dressing.

Makes 4-6 servings.

Fun Facts
The President has five major jobs: to head up the nation's armed forces; to appoint people to certain government positions; to handle foreign affairs, including signing treaties with other countries; to sign or veto laws, and to see that laws are enforced, including laws that make sure eggs are safe to eat!

20

Justice's Jigglin' Fruit Salad

1 package lemon Jell-O®
1 package orange Jell-O®
2 8 oz. cans pineapple
   chunks, drained
2 cups green grapes
1/3 cup mini-marshmallows
2 bananas, sliced
3 1/2 cups very hot water
Whipped cream (optional)

You will need:

Knife
Measuring cup
Wooden spoon
Large bowl

Dissolve Jell-O® in 3 1/2 cups very hot water, stirring with wooden spoon. Cool completely. When cool, add fruit and marshmallows and mix. Refrigerate until firm. Top servings with whipped cream if desired.

Fun Facts

The Supreme Court has nine justices and is the highest court in the land, with the final power to interpret the U.S. Constitution. It picks its cases very carefully. Each year, the Court gets 7,000 requests, or petitions, to hear a case. But the Court only wants to hear the most important of them, so it usually agrees to consider just 90 to 100 cases during a term, which begins each year on the first Monday in October.

Red, White and Green Room Salad

2 cups (8 oz.) bowtie pasta
1 cup mayonnaise
1/4 cup chopped onion
1/2 cup sliced celery
1/3 cup chopped
   red pepper
1 teaspoon sugar
1 teaspoon salt
1/4 teaspoon pepper
2 tablespoons cider vinegar
1 teaspoon yellow mustard
   (optional)

You will need:

Sauce pan and water
Knife to chop
Cutting board
Measuring cup and spoons
Large bowl and spoon

Cook pasta according to package directions, rinse and drain. Combine mayonnaise, vinegar, mustard (if using), sugar, salt and pepper in large bowl. Add pasta, red pepper, onion and celery. Toss to coat. Chill covered in refrigerator.

Makes 6 servings.

Fun Facts

In the White House, the Red room is one of four reception rooms. In the 1800s, it was used mainly as a music room. During the administration of our fourth president, James Madison, it was yellow! The Green Room is another reception room. But the third president, Thomas Jefferson, used it as a dining room. Both rooms were renovated in 1971.

Breads

2 cups flour

1 tablespoon baking powder

8 tablespoons unsalted
   butter, softened

1/2 cup sugar

1 egg

1/2 teaspoon salt

1/2 teaspoon ground nutmeg

1 teaspoon vanilla extract

1 lb. very ripe bananas

1/4 cup chopped pecans

Bureaucrat's Banana Bread

You will need:

Electric mixer
Measuring cup and spoons
Loaf pan, greased
Flour sifter

Cream together butter and sugar with electric mixer until fluffy. Add egg and beat thoroughly. Sift together flour, baking powder and nutmeg and set aside. Mash together bananas and vanilla extract. Add flour mixture and banana mixture alternately to butter mixture, beating after each addition until blended. Add pecans and mix well. Pour batter into greased loaf pan. Bake at 350 degrees for one hour.

Fun Facts

A bureaucrat is a person who works in a government department, office or bureau, such as the Department of Education or the Bureau of the Mint, which makes coins. Bureaucrats live all around the country and make sure that the work of the government gets done.

22

Orange Liberty Loaf

You will need:

Loaf pan, greased
Measuring cup
Measuring spoons
Grater

2 cups all purpose flour

3/4 cup sugar

2 teaspoons baking powder

3/4 teaspoon salt

1/2 teaspoon baking soda

1 egg, beaten

1/4 cup oil

1 teaspoon grated orange peel

2/3 cup orange juice

Mix together first five ingredients and set aside. Add oil, orange peel and orange juice to beaten egg. Add egg mixture to dry mixture, mixing only enough to moisten dry mixture. Grease bottom and sides of a loaf pan. Pour bread mixture into pan. Bake at 350 degrees for 1 hour. Cool completely on rack before slicing. You can also glaze before slicing.

Glaze:
1/2 cup confectioners sugar
2 1/2 teaspoons orange juice,
1 teaspoon grated orange peel

Place confectioners sugar in small bowl. Stir in orange juice until smooth. Add orange peel and mix well. Drizzle over loaf.

Fun Facts

Liberty is defined as the ability to make free choices and carry them out. Political liberty gives people the right to participate in the formation of their government; it includes the right to vote and to run for office. Social liberty includes freedom of speech and freedom of religion.

"Liberty" was the name of the dog belonging to Gerald Ford, the 38th president.

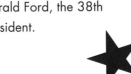

Inaugu-raisin Apple Biscuits

You will need:

Measuring cup and spoons
Mixing bowl
Spoon
Vegetable peeler
Grater
Cookie sheet, greased

2 cups prepared biscuit mix
2 tablespoons sugar
1/2 teaspoon cinnamon
1/4 teaspoon nutmeg
1/2 cup raisins
1 small red apple, shredded
1/2 cup milk

Mix together biscuit mix, sugar, cinnamon and nutmeg in bowl. Add raisins and stir. Peel skin from apple and shred with hand held grater until only the core is left. Add apple to biscuit mixture. Pour milk into mixing bowl with biscuit mixture. Stir until mixture is moist, but lumpy. Drop mixture by rounded spoonfuls onto greased cookie sheet. Bake at 450 degrees for 10-12 minutes or until golden. Serve immediately.

Makes 10-12 biscuits.

Fun Facts

"Inaugu-raisin" is a pun of the word "inauguration." The presidential inauguration is the ceremony held January 20th every four years to officially induct the president-elect into office. The president-elect is "sworn in" by the Chief Justice of the Supreme Court, on the steps of the Capitol. Inauguration Day is marked with parties and parades honoring the new president and his family.

Cloakroom Corn Muffins

You will need:

Measuring cup and spoons
Bowls
Muffin tin
Spoon
Muffin cup liners

1 cup sweet corn
1 cup buttermilk
1/4 cup oil
2 tablespoons molasses
1 tablespoon brown sugar
1 egg, beaten
3/4 cup yellow cornmeal
1/2 cup flour
2 teaspoons baking powder
1/4 teaspoon salt
1/2 teaspoon baking soda

Place liners in muffin tin. Combine corn, buttermilk, oil, molasses, brown sugar and egg in a bowl. In a small bowl, mix together cornmeal, flour, baking powder, baking soda and salt. Stir flour mixture into corn mixture until just blended. Do not overmix. Pour batter into muffin cups, filling up 2/3 full. Bake about 15 minutes at 400 degrees until muffins are browned.

Makes 12 muffins.

Fun Facts

The Capital has several cloakrooms, small rooms off of the floors of the House and Senate where lawmakers can relax, meet and talk in private. There is a cloakroom in each chamber for members of each political party–Democratic cloakrooms and Republican cloakrooms.

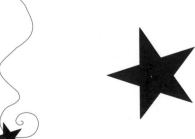

25

Drinks

Secret Service Sarsaparilla Floats

Vanilla ice cream
Root beer
Whipped cream
Maraschino cherries

You will need:

Tall glass
Ice cream scoop
Long spoon
Straw

Put two scoops of vanilla ice cream in a tall glass. Pour root beer slowly over ice cream. Top with whipped cream or another small scoop of ice cream and a cherry. Serve with a long spoon and a straw.

Fun Facts

The Secret Service is the federal law enforcement agency that is assigned primarily to protect the president. It was organized in 1865 to fight counterfeiting. It began protecting the president and his family in 1901, after the assassination of President William McKinley.

Pentagon Punch

1 12 oz. can frozen cranberry
    juice concentrate
3/4 cup orange juice
1 quart seltzer water or
    ginger ale, chilled
1 bag frozen raspberries
1 orange, sliced
1 lemon, sliced

You will need:

Punch bowl and ladle
Measuring cup
Knife
Cutting board

Thaw cranberry juice concentrate. Combine cranberry juice, orange juice and pour into punch bowl. Pour frozen raspberries into punch. Slice lemon and orange and add slices to punch. Chill. Add seltzer or ginger ale just before serving.

Makes 8-10 servings.

Fun Facts

The Pentagon is one of the largest office buildings in the world. Located across the Potomac River in Northern Virginia, it is the headquarters of the U.S. military. It is a five-sided structure (a pentagon), covers 29 acres and holds more than 20,000 employees.

Mouse-jority Leader's Lemonade

4 cups water

3/4 cup sugar

3/4 cup freshly squeezed
lemon juice (about 3 lemons)

1/2 cup freshly squeezed
orange juice (about 2 oranges)

Lemon and orange slices
for garnish

You will need:

Hand-held or electric juicer
Cutting board
Knife
Measuring cup
Pitcher
Long spoon

Hold citrus juicer over 2 cup measuring cup. Cut lemons and oranges in half through the middle. Rotate on the citrus juicer, pushing down to get all the juice. Pour lemon and orange juice into a pitcher. Add the water and sugar. Stir all ingredients together until sugar dissolves. Pour into glasses over ice. Garnish with fruit slices.

Makes 4 servings.

Fun Facts

"Mouse-jority Leader" is a play-on-words of the phrase "Majority Leader." The Majority Leader is the chief legislative officer of the Senate. He is usually the leader of the party in control of the chamber, the majority party.

Senate Smoothies

2 bananas

1 cup strawberries

1 cup plain yogurt

1 tablespoon sugar or
1 1/2 tablespoons honey

1 teaspoon vanilla flavoring
(optional)

You will need:

Measuring cup and spoons
Blender

Combine all ingredients in blender. Blend until smooth.

Makes 2 servings.

Fun Facts

The Senate is made up of 100 members, two from each of the 50 states. They serve six-year terms. The Vice President serves as President of the Senate and votes in the event of a tie. In order for a bill to become a law, the Senate, as well as the House of Representatives, must approve it.

Desserts

- 1 box prepared brownie mix
- 1/2 cup semi-sweet chocolate chips
- 1/2 cup mini-mousemallows
- 1 cup chopped Baby Ruth® bars (about 3 candy bars)

Baby Ruth Brownies

You will need:

Ingredients for brownie mix
Baking dish

Foil
Spoon
Measuring cup
Knife

Chop Baby Ruth® bars into small pieces. Prepare brownie mix according to package directions. Stir in chocolate chips. Pour mixture into baking dish. Sprinkle top of brownie mixture with Baby Ruth® pieces until lightly covered. Bake according to directions. When done, remove from oven. Sprinkle mini-mousemallows and remaining Baby Ruth® pieces on top of brownies. Cover with foil for 15 minutes. Cool before cutting.

Fun Facts

Contrary to popular belief, the Baby Ruth® candy bar was not named after Babe Ruth, the famous baseball player. It was actually named after the daughter of President Grover Cleveland's first child, Ruth.

First Lady Fingers

Mix: chocolate chips, sprinkles, candy bar pieces, strawberries, bananas, etc., into any one of these:

Peanut butter
Marshmallow cream
Pudding
Cool whip®
Frosting

You will need:

1 package store-bought lady fingers
Your choice of toppings and mix-ins.

Either slice lady fingers down the middle or put your choice of mixture directly on top of lady fingers.

Fun Facts

The wife of the president was first called the "First Lady" during the administration of our 19th president, Rutherford B. Hayes; the name was given to his wife, Lucy. There is no formal description of the job of the First Lady in the Constitution or anywhere else. Aside from serving as official hostess at the White House, each First Lady can make the position anything she wants.

Marshall's Supreme Torte

You will need:

2 9-inch round cake pans
Measuring cups
Ingredients for cake mix
Knife
Flour for cake pans
Spoon
Cake plate

1 package yellow cake mix

2/3 cup strawberry jam

3 cups fresh strawberries,
    sliced

8 oz. frozen whipped topping,
    thawed and divided

1/4 cup chocolate syrup

Grease and flour two 9-inch round
cake pans. Mix and bake cake layers
according to package directions.
Cool completely. Place one cake
layer on plate. Spread with 1/3 cup
strawberry jam. Arrange 1 cup
strawberries on jam. Drizzle with
chocolate syrup. Spread half the
whipped cream over strawberries.
Place second cake layer on top.
Repeat with remaining strawberry
jam, 1 cup strawberries, and
whipped topping. Top with remaining 1 cup strawberries and drizzle
with chocolate syrup. Refrigerate
until ready to serve.

Makes about 12 servings.

Fun Facts

The Supreme Court today
is made up of one chief
justice and eight associate
justices. But it wasn't always
that way. Congress decides
how many justices should
sit on the Court, and the
number has varied from
five in 1789 to as many
as 10 in 1863. The Court
has had nine members
since 1869.

Dolley Madison's Ice Cream Sundaes

You will need:

Sundae or parfait glasses
  (or a tall glass)
Ice cream scoop
Knife

Vanilla ice cream

Chocolate sauce

Caramel sauce

100 Grand® candy bar pieces
  (about 2 bars)

Whipped cream (optional)

Maraschino cherries
  (optional)

Chop 100 Grand® bars into small pieces. Put one small scoop of ice cream in glass. Squirt desired amount of chocolate sauce over ice cream and follow with a sprinkle of 100 Grand® bar pieces. Repeat using caramel sauce. Top with final scoop of ice cream. (Add whipped cream now, if using.) Drizzle top with chocolate and caramel sauce. Sprinkle with remaining 100 Grand® bar pieces. Top with cherry.

Makes 4 sundaes.

30

Fun Facts

Dolley Madison, wife of the fourth president, James Madison, was the Capital's best hostess in the early days of the nation. She was the first First Lady to serve ice cream in the White House.

Capitol Crunch Bars

You will need:

Heavy saucepan
Measuring cup
Wooden spoon
Square baking dish
Knife
Spatula

1 (14 oz.) package caramels

1/4 cup milk

4 cups Rice Krispies® cereal

1 cup salted peanuts

Shortening or butter for
    greasing dish

Unwrap caramels and place in heavy saucepan. Add milk. Cook and stir, over low heat, with wooden spoon until caramels are melted, about 15 minutes. Remove pan from burner. Add Rice Krispies® and peanuts to caramel mixture. Stir until well coated. Grease baking dish on bottom and sides. Spoon cereal mixture into dish and press down with the back of the spoon. Let mixture stand about 1 hour, or until firm. Cut mixture into squares and serve.

Makes about 16 squares.

Fun Facts

The Capitol is the home of the legislative branch of the government, the House of Representatives and the Senate. George Washington laid the cornerstone for the building in 1793, but the structure was not fully completed until 1826, after the construction of the domed center. It covers 16.5 acres and has 540 rooms, 658 windows and 850 doorways.

Blue Room Berry Boats

You will need:

Knife
Cutting board
Bowls
Measuring cup and spoons
Mixer

3/4 cup blueberries

3/4 cup raspberries

1 cup sliced bananas

1 cantaloupe

1 cup heavy cream

2 tablespoons sugar

1/4 teaspoon cinnamon

1/2 teaspoon vanilla extract

Wash blueberries and raspberries. Pat dry. Slice banana and combine the three in a bowl. Cut cantaloupe in half and remove seeds. Cut the halves in half and then in quarters, to make 8 slices. Remove rind. This will be the boat. Beat whipping cream in a large bowl with sugar, cinnamon and vanilla until soft peaks form. Spoon berry mixture into center of boat and top with whipped cream.

Makes 8 small boats – or simply quarter cantaloupe for 4 larger boats.

32

Fun Facts:

The Blue Room, the oval room in the center of the main floor of the White House, is another reception room in the mansion. The first president to occupy the White House, John Adams, briefly used it as an entryway. It is most famous for being the room that holds the White House Christmas Tree each year.